Good People... Bad Marriages

Wisdom to Know.. Freedom to Choose..
Courage to Change

by

Marsha Lee Hudgens

Love is definable, the same in any application, parental, friendly, romantic, universal. It becomes complex and confusing when we make up our own self-serving definition for it.

♂ 🖐🖐 ♀

ESTUARY PUBLISHING 1996

Good People; Bad Marriages

Library of Congress Catalog Card Number: 96-96505

Hudgens, Marsha L., Good People; Bad Marriages
Wisdom to Know-Freedom to Choose-Courage to Change
ISBN 0-9653075-2-2 : $13.95

Printed in the United States of America

Cover design by Ryan Hale, Adeas Graphics, Sparta, TN.

If unavailable in bookstores, additional copies of this book may be purchased by using the order form included in the back or by contacting the publisher at the above address. For quicker service, fax: (615) 446-2912

CONTENTS

Climbing the Wall

Just because most people believe something, doesn't mean it's true. Misconceptions about love, marriage and divorce are not instilled in us in ways so obvious that we can argue with them. Conditioning, subtle and constant from birth, to get into and stay in a marriage is strong, regardless of the quality of the union.

Marriage is great for the ego. Having a permanent partner says to the rest of the world that somebody wants us enough to commit to us for a lifetime. It's a public declaration of our acceptability. If we get to be twenty-five or thirty and that hasn't happened, we're made to believe there must be something terribly wrong with us. People begin to wonder what that is. *We* begin to wonder what that is.

No matter what your age, if you haven't met someone with whom you're absolutely certain you want to spend seventy years, there could be something very right with you. You may be more right than eighty percent of the population. More than half of all marriages end in divorce, another twenty percent probably should.

Divorce is more common today than it was twenty or thirty years ago, but the stigma attached to it is still there. We've all heard the mounting divorce rate explained by phrases similar to this one: "People just don't try as hard or care as much as they used to." I don't believe that's true. And even if it were, in the case of bad marriages, it would be a good thing.

My experience with divorce was vastly different from what I had feared it would be. I remained in a bad marriage years more than I should have for all the reasons other people do. Thanks to one wonderful, opened minded friend who pointed out the senselessness of it, I'm now free.

I wasted years listening to experts, leaders and 'wise' older marrieds. They all said, "Marriage is right, stay in it, work at it. Divorce is wrong, stay away from it." My marriage never seemed right and years of hard work didn't make it better.

I wish I had known that since the majority of marriages are not right, the majority of divorces are not wrong. It seems illogical to me now, but like most people, I didn't realize divorces are unjustifiably blamed for problems created by bad marriages and the mental instability of individual marital partners.

When others saw my post-divorce transformation, they began to talk and ask questions. It seemed men and women of all ages tried to negotiate in a world of relationships which had been made alien to them by ignorant instruction. I saw many in bad marriages who felt as trapped as I had. I wanted to tell them divorce isn't bad, in fact, it's much more than worth the effort. I wanted to reach those who were about to become trapped, to prevent it if possible. I wanted to reach those who, by thoughtlessly advising, reinforced false beliefs and helped impose imprisonment for a large sector of the population.

Since bad marriages can happen to anyone, I deliberately switched genders in the following paragraphs. This could be someone you know.

"Night after night I sit in a room with a stranger. During the day we're away from each other. Most nights I'm stuck. This is home. I have no other place to go. If she wasn't breathing, I wouldn't know she was alive. Not that I care. Sometimes I hate the way she breathes. I don't much like the way she does anything."

"I don't care that he's not talking. It has been a long time since I wanted to hear what he has to say. I usually disagree with him anyway. Obviously, he doesn't care to talk with me either. Sometimes I think dying would be better than this. I wonder if my health problems aren't an unconscious desire to accomplish that very thing. In spite of feeling guilty about it, I catch myself hoping he'll die first so I'll have a few years of freedom or I wish he wouldn't come home or that I didn't have to come home to him."

"Over the years, I've tried everything to make it better. Sometimes it worked for a while. But it was never quite right, never optimum. Something was always missing. Even when it was the best, I talked myself through it. "Yes, this is good. See? This marriage isn't always bad. Remember good times like these instead of always dwelling on the bad times. It's better than being alone. We've been through the worst of it. It'll be okay from here on. She isn't a really bad person. I do love her.... sometimes... in a way. Maybe I'm just not trying hard enough."

"But now I've reached the point where I don't care enough to try anymore. I don't pretend as well as I used to. I've felt like a hypocrite for a long time, like I'm trapped in a badly written play. I've simply resigned myself to living above and in spite of my marriage. How depressing to think of retirement or being buried beside him. I feel I've been buried beside him most of my life."

"I cope with it, quiet on the outside, turbulent on

the inside. I don't know what else to do. Bad times have become less tolerable. There are no more good times with her. I close myself off to good relationships by giving so much time and emotional energy to this one. What choice do I have? I endure low grade discontent a few weeks and months at a time, too tired from it to fight it. Months turn into years."

"The years will become my life. Before I die, I may spend sixty or seventy years with him, what a waste. I hate him for the bondage he represents. The children won't come around much when we're old. They're already tired of the bickering and bitterness. It'll just be him and me. And I'll never know freedom until I die."

♂ ☜📖☞ ♀

It doesn't have to happen. It doesn't take bad people to make a bad marriage. It takes two people who don't belong together, who married for the wrong reasons. Love was never sufficient or truly mutual. People force themselves to live together without love and force always produces pressure. Pressure must be relieved. Relief manifests itself as mental, verbal and sometimes physical abuse directed at our spouse, or worse, the children.

We think if we've put ten to twenty years into it, we're expected to keep it going. If we've stood it for thirty or forty years, we might as well finish out our life in it. If we have nothing *really big* to present as our justification for *throwing it all away,* we fear taking steps to change it. *I've never been happy,* seems like a weak excuse for such drastic action. But how drastic is it?

Sometimes it's moving to a different place or maybe adjusting your schedule to include child visitation. It's sorting and dividing property. It's having one legal document nullified by another legal document.

I may be oversimplifying, but I hardly counterbalance the masses who perplex and instill in us our unfounded fears, doubts and constricting beliefs about marital relationships.

None of us expect to be happy just because we marry. What we hope for, what we deserve, is predominant peace and contentment, within our homes and more importantly, within ourselves. I encourage you to objectively observe as many relationships as possible so you can make a comparative judgement about the validity of what I present here.

On the following pages I have disclosed ideas and information from as many sources as I could absorb, countless personal talks, experience, observations, interviews, mass communication data, and a survey I circulated to hundreds of people. I sought both positive and negative sides to prevent my views from being as biased as those I had always heard.

One survey was for married persons whom had been married for at least twenty years to the same spouse, and one was for divorced persons whom had been married for at least ten years to the same spouse. I enlisted the help of friends, relatives, acquaintances, strangers and OnLine America in circulating the surveys. The participants didn't have to be happy or unhappy, male or female, wealthy or not, educated or not, religious or not, or any particular race.

Armed with the truth, we can master our fate in an

area where majority opinion and advice is narrow and information is distorted. We have options and choices. There is such a thing as a good marriage. Perhaps, just as we demand quality by returning shoddy merchandise, there would be *only* good marriages if we didn't so passively settle for less.

We can't avoid making decisions.
When we do nothing, we've made the
decision to do nothing.....

Running On Empty

We are our minds, our spirits and our bodies. We all know what our minds and our bodies include. Our spirit isn't so familiar.

It's the animating vital principal, our heart and soul, a supernatural essence that gives intuition, sensitivity, inspiration, compassion, love and life to our mind and body. It doesn't regard time or distance. It's ageless, enthusiastic, curious, adventurous, playful, carefree, trusting, giving and honest. It is childlike in it's openness. Not only is it the thing in us that impels us to love others, it's the thing in us that others love.

When I use the term spirit or spiritual, it will be in that context. It's not to be confused with religion or religious which is or has to do with the worship of a deity. Though some have spirits more constricted by negativity, everyone has a spirit and is therefore spiritual. Not everyone is religious.

We *outwardly express* love with our bodies and our minds. We can also use them to deny and constrict our spirit by behaving contrarily to what we feel, denying our feelings and/or trying to change how we feel. If our mind-set is in opposition to our spiritual inclination, we'll have inner conflict.

The spirit should lead us. It's on a vast superior plane of intelligence. It draws knowledge and power from infinity. It can neither be controlled nor does it control us. It makes suggestions by means of intuition which guides us toward positive goals. The more faith and dependency we show it, the more effective it is. But it demands nothing. The spirit's inclinations often go against what our minds have spent years learning, musts and mustn'ts, shoulds and shouldn'ts, cans and can'ts, needs and needn'ts.

Our mind is a time keeper, a calculator, an analyzer, a cause and effect computer, totally limited to mortal reasoning and above all, a controller. It decides whether or not to follow the suggestions our spirit makes. It asks what, why, when, where and how, then replies with the answers. It doesn't like change or to be changed.

Change requires reprogramming. It's synonymous with being too stupid to get it right the first time, being inconsistent, frivolous and undependable. If we do change our mind, we must justify, excuse and explain until we're sufficiently exonerated.

Our mind defines our needs, comes up with a plan and uses that plan to demand action. It's automatic and self-motivated. It's in charge when we're born and becomes more skilled as we grow. When we were infants we knew that if we cried (demand) our mother rushed in with food and a dry diaper (response).

The only true emotions our mind produces are demanding, such as anger, jealousy and frustration. All

13

other mind produced emotions are an act, learned characterizations of the real thing utilized to incite reaction.

Our spirit needs our mind and body to function in a mortal world. The mind should follow and aid the spirit, though once we reach adulthood, it seldom does. Our mind *learns* to fear. We fear our spirit because it can't be explained. It's too vast for our mind to comprehend. As we gain reasoning knowledge from other minds and become more intelligent, our mind denies the existence of anything beyond its own supremacy.

Suppose your spirit strongly suggests you'd be happy going around the world on a sail boat. It suggests there's an infinite reason for you to follow that dream. Your mind may tell you it's impractical and impossible, just a foolish fantasy and nothing good could come of it. It may give you negatives until you finally shelve the idea. You stay where you are and unhappily do what you *should* do the rest of your life. That would be your mind overpowering your spirit and taking control.

Suppose instead, after much analyzing and

reasoning, your mind heeds the spirit and says go for it. It then determines what you'll have to do, how much it will cost, and devises ways to make it happen. You sail around the world, happier than you ever imagined being. You meet hundreds of people and because you're positive, you touch many lives in a positive way. Spirit leads; mind and body aid.

Lowest in intelligence on our self organizational chart is the body, the machine governed by our two superior components and automatically produced chemicals. Except for warning us of maintenance problems, we shouldn't allow our bodies to greatly influence any major decisions, and yet we do. In too many cases our minds and bodies decide we *should* get married and to whom. The spirit's vote is ignored. Since we only use two of the necessary three components and neither of them was the most important, we create a doomed marriage.

A bad marriage suppresses, oppresses, depresses and drains all three components. As the years pass, we escape real feeling more and more. We're out of balance.

15

Good People... Bad Marriages

Our spirit is constricted. Our mind is burdened with the great effort of denial. Our bodies deteriorate more rapidly.

Because we've become actors, we go about our daily lives pretending to be content. We focus outwardly and talk about things our minds can explain, physical illnesses, the weather and other people, safe, scientific, logical things. We don't talk about our marriages, our main source of inner turmoil. If someone brings it up, we lie, make a joke, pretend it doesn't matter or say what everyone expects us to say.

Our spirit rebels and pleads for justice. It prompts us to tell the truth and live it. We fear rebellion. Rebellion causes conflict, the very thing we try so hard to avoid. Yet in a bad marriage, we live in conflict every day, whether it's the war going on inside us between our minds and spirits or the war going on in our homes.

The battle rages for years. Our mind solicits and receives help from other minds. It repeatedly batters the spirit with majority opinion and learned negativity. Our spirit becomes tired, frustrated and too weak to rally. When that happens, we become old, empty and apathetic.

This can happen at a very young physical age and continue until we die.

Any type of relationship has the potential to be spirit numbing. If true contentment is to be achieved, spirit damaging relationships should be eliminated from our lives or minimized to the greatest extent possible. In adulthood, we always have a choice.

True happiness is having all three life components operating at peak efficiency and in the proper order of authority. We nurture and trust the spirit. We teach and utilize the mind. We nourish and exercise the body.

This brings us to the four possible planes of bonding that lead to marriage. They are arranged in the most common order of importance in which we place them when we choose a mate.

I. Neediness bonding - Our desire to fulfill our own psychological needs and our perception of how well our chosen partner can do it. These needs are determined by our personalities and the environment in which we were raised. Though they are powerful driving forces, they're

17

usually unconscious and undefined. Therefore, we couple them with physical attraction and mistakenly define them as love.

Needs change as we grow older. Sometimes we grow completely out of our neediness. Either condition alters the way we relate to others. If our marriage is based on neediness, it seldom survives the transition.

For a more in depth study of this type of relationship, read the books written by Robin Norwood. Whether you're a woman or a man, you'll recognize the part you play in forming a doomed union.

II. Physical bonding - Physical attraction and sexual activities. Often this is more important or equal in importance to neediness bonding when we choose a partner.

III. Legal - Marriage license, written documentation, good until death or legal absolution.

IV. Spiritual - True love, that magic thing that isn't really magic. The most important but most frequently misunderstood or ignored. In a bad marriage, the most frequently and seriously lacking in one or both partners.

Love is definable. Love is the same in any application, parental, friendly, romantic, universal. Hereinafter, when I use the term love or true love it will be by the following definition in its purest form. It will include neither physical attraction nor neediness bonding.

Love is *always* honest, dependable, considerate, compassionate, sensitive, affectionate, trusting, trustworthy, optimistic, patient, kind, humble and generous. It's produced by a wholly giving spirit.

Love is *never* superficial, selfish, critical, indifferent, angry, jealous, suspicious, deceitful, competitive, arrogant, controlling or cruel. These are all products of a needy mind. We may feel and exhibit these negative traits but they are never produced by love. How these positive and negative traits balance tell us how much love is in our marriage.

Love isn't complex and confusing. It becomes that

19

when we make up our own self-serving definition for it. *We can't make ourselves feel it. We can't make ourselves not feel it.* On a level above mortal reason and control, it is given and received spiritually. From infinity it draws its awesome strength.

In a good marriage as in life, all three components operate efficiently, *mutually* and in proper order. Our love is sustained and nourished through our spirits. Our minds are curious and stimulated intellectually. Our bodies are appreciated and satisfied sexually. We grow separately as whole individuals and together as a unit, and the growth continues throughout our lives.

We can be different from our partner in many ways, but we must give and receive from all three components in balance with our partner. If any one is lacking, we may have many things, an arrangement, a marriage license, a marriage of convenience, a roommate, a friend or an enemy. We do not have a good marriage.

A good marriage is the same as anything good. It should comfort us and give us peace. We should be who we are without fear, suppression or conflict, external or internal. We shouldn't have to pretend or talk ourselves through it. Problems should be solved with *mutual* respect, understanding and sacrifice, products of love.

Marriage is not give and take. Taking has no place in a relationship, whether we're taking someone's freedom, strength and self-respect or taking their abuse. Love is a giving thing. Though it never demands reciprocation, if it isn't equally reciprocated, it can't grow and will eventually become dormant or destroyed.

They (scientists) suffer from a kind of tunnel vision, a psychologically self-imposed .... set of blinders which prevents them from turning their attention to the realm of the spirit.

M. Scott Peck, M.D. from *The Road Less Traveled*

Courting up a Storm

Prevention of any mistake is the ideal approach. But we don't know we're about to enter a bad marriage even when there are telling signs. We simply don't know what they are or we ignore them.

We're on our very best behavior during courtship, trying to impress. Many people think once they're married, they don't have to try any more. Any slight problems we encounter during courtship are likely to develop into huge ones after marriage.

Jealousy that's a little flattering while you're dating will become an affront to your faithfulness. You'll wonder why you even try if you'll be accused anyway, or you'll withdraw socially in an effort to appease your mate. Little flairs of temper you think are cute and show passion will become a source of fear. To prevent anger, you'll avoid doing things you'd really like to do, or you'll become sneaky and dislike yourself for it.

The neatness you think will be a nice balance for your sloppiness will become a control point for both of you. Concern about and careful attention to appearance will become vanity and pretentiousness.

Little white lies will become big black ones when you're the one to whom they're being told. Cruelty and criticism directed at someone else will soon be directed at you. Ambition will become neglect. You'll feel unimportant compared to his or her career.

What looks laid back and carefree in the dating days will look like laziness after a few years of marriage. Spontaneity is likely to become careless impulsiveness. Compliancy will become spinelessness. One who's fostering and assertive will quickly seem domineering and overbearing. Preoccupation with physical symptoms may

24

be evidence of hypochondria. A slight weight problem is likely to blossom into obesity, and so on. What you see may be what you get, times a thousand.

Love for others means acceptance of them the way they are. Unfortunately, we don't know how much we'll have to accept until we live with someone a few years. What then? Is it commitment or confinement? Which is really worse, staying in or getting out?

Though I use the following survey questions for form and simplification, the answers came from *all* my sources. When I say most or the majority, I mean seventy to ninety-five percent. Percentages are close approximates. I sometimes distinguish happily from unhappily married people based on how often they considered divorce, whether or not love was apparent in the marriage, how problems were dealt with and answers to other pertinent questions.

I estimated twenty percent of my married sources are truly in good marriages, thirty percent are in questionable marriages and denying it, and the remaining fifty percent are definitely in bad marriages. Because their responses were contradictory, answers from those in confusion and denial will push percentages thirty percent either way.

If questions were similar on both surveys, I combined them. They evolved from ideas expressed by those with whom I communicated. Some of the questions were poorly stated (my fault, never intentional). The respondents let me know about it. For example: "How often in your marriage were you completely satisfied with your spouse?" Some participants returned with "What's *completely* satisfied!?!" and simply "Never!". I sensed understandable agitation in those exclamation points.

All answers are briefly outlined. Areas of more concern will be discussed more fully than others, such as how children are affected, why we wait so long to act, the divorce process, etc. We will explore love, marriage and divorce relationships, good and bad, from courtship to two years beyond dissolution. Through the experiences of many, we will see ourselves and those we love. The survey questions are in bold.

1. When you married, how old were you?

The most common answer was *19-21 with 22-25 running second.* A few were *in their mid-teens;* a few were *in their thirties.*

Age isn't a determining factor in producing a bad marriage if the marriage lasts more than ten years. Even some who marry in their teens can be lucky enough to find the right mate. And those who marry in their thirties or after can marry the wrong person.

Apparently, we don't know what we're doing at any age. Many of the best marriages come about by random good fortune. If we're older when we get married, and it lasts more than ten years or it's our second marriage, it's a little more difficult to come up with an excuse to end it. And we do need a good excuse, don't we?

27

2. How long before the marriage did you know your fiancee well and how long did you date?

These answers ranged from years to months with no obvious relevancy to the quality of the marriage.

Most answers disclosed the time between initial acquaintance and marriage during which we're more familiar with our fiancees. About half the married participants and we who are divorced apparently *never* know our spouses *well*. We also feel they really don't know or understand us.

3. What was your first impression of this person?

"Thought he/she was attractive, interesting, " was the most common answer among both married and divorced.

"...Didn't like much.. ..Not impressed..." ran a distant second. This was about equal for all, married or divorced,

but *none* of the happily marrieds answered this way.

"...*Knew this was it (love) when we met...*" was least common but very close to second. And interestingly, all these answers came from happily marrieds. Don't confuse this statement with: "Had a feeling this was the person I was going to marry." (No mention of love.) Some of those answers came from divorced people.

4. How long did you date before you knew you were in love?

The most common range here was three to six months with other ranges going from minutes to years. The only consistent pattern was in the minutes and the happily marrieds.

Love at first sight is *extremely* rare. Strong physical attraction can easily be mistaken for it. Don't do something impulsive because you think you're experiencing it. All these people dated for several months

29

to be sure, even after that sensational first meeting.

5. Why did you love this particular person?

All participants, married and divorced, stated lovable traits. Their fiancees were *dependable, considerate, generous, sensitive, fun, exciting, etc., etc., etc.....*

Notice how quickly our minds throw out reasons if we're asked for them. In fact, we can't explain why we love one person in particular when any number of people may have the same qualities. Some say it's a matter of availability, but that seldom proves true.

If we do choose a spouse based mostly on practical reasons, and we don't love them all that much to begin with, we think we'll grow to love them more. We've been told love grows, that it isn't an instant feeling. But it doesn't always grow. And it can be an instant feeling.

6. Have you ever been in love with anyone else? If yes, how many times?

50% *had never considered themselves in love with anyone besides their spouse.*

About 40% *had been in love only one other time.* Less than 10% *had been in love more than twice.*

7. Compare your feelings for this person(s) with your feelings for your spouse.

In all cases, *the feelings for the other person were more passionate.*

Since not many of us know what love is, do we really love only once, or do we ever? Do we allow circumstances, impatience and emotional instability to prevent real love from culminating?

31

Good People... Bad Marriages

When we're young, perhaps we fear the powerful bonding that real love produces. In love, we feel out of control, powerless, vulnerable. We want to give everything to and for another person. Unconsciously, our neediness rebels against such unselfishness. Our childish insecurities won't allow us to feel worthy of being loved so much. We couldn't bear to disappoint, or to allow ourselves love so deeply, then possibly lose it. We devastate the relationship before it devastates us.

Our reasoning mind convinces us to leave it and find someone who'll meet our needs, for whom we can control our feelings and with whom we'll feel more powerful. We don't fear being hurt and we don't worry so much about hurting. Our bodies help convince us we can have sexual fulfillment with anyone. We usually think we love the person we're marrying by the time the wedding date arrives. Our spirit is telling us just how true that love is whether or not our mind agrees.

Sometimes people marry first, then find themselves falling in love with someone else. They may feel a stronger bond with the other person, but they're married.

Now there's more conflict than ever. They often complicate matters by having an affair.

They have to hide something they want to shout to the world. They feel guilty, ashamed and frustrated. Everything is wrong when everything should be right. They lose respect for and trust in themselves and their lover. If the affair is found out, they may lose the respect of those dear to them.

We can prevent the tragedy by waiting, learning about healthy relationships, becoming balanced ourselves and letting our spirit lead us into the right relationship or none at all. If we're in a bad marriage, we can begin the journey to personal balance and if necessary, get out of our marriage.

Don't be deceived, *good marriage partners* don't have multiple affairs. A partner *from a good marriage* doesn't have an affair at all. And affairs *never* make a marriage better.

8. In the weeks and days before the wedding, what doubts did you have?

None.
Married: 50%
Divorced: 5%

Wondered if I could handle the responsibility.

Married: 30%
Divorced: 5%

Wondered if we should wait. Wondered if I should marry this person.

Married: 20%
Divorced: 90%

Note the doubts expressed by most of the divorced. Even if we're very doubtful as the wedding draws near, we don't usually back out. We go ahead for some of the same reasons we stay in it:

> **Apathy:**   Backing out is too much trouble, especially if a big wedding is planned.
>
> **Low expectations:** We expect to have doubts.
>
> **Shame or Pride:** We hate to admit mistakes.
>
> **Confusion:** Inner turmoil. We don't know what's right.
>
> **Emotional instability:** We still want our needs to be met.
>
> **Sense of responsibility:** We said we'd do it.
>
> **Pressure**: If we back out a lot of people will be upset. We'll have to deal with friends, family and a fiancee who will be hurt, humiliated and angry.

Don't marry thinking if it doesn't work, you'll end it. You have serious doubts going in. Marriage tends to generate ties of the familial and financial kind that can be very binding. The longer you're married the more binding they become.

If you don't have the strength of character to refuse to marry when you have doubts, you won't have enough to end the marriage. Enduring a bad marriage is a poor way to strengthen character. It's more likely to strengthen negativity and lower self-esteem.

If you think living together first is the best preventive measure, your need based mind is in control. Living together can create all the binders a marriage can except the legal.

Don't talk yourself into either one. Above all, don't let someone else talk you into it. You'll be talking yourself through it for years, maybe for the rest of your life. Even fifteen years with the wrong person is a big ugly chunk of your life.

Date different people. Dating a singular person before you're absolutely sure you love them is a sign of immaturity and insecurity (neediness). Remain free in case the right partner does come along. When that happens, you'll have no doubts. If you're thinking about marriage, think carefully. And don't be afraid to change your mind. It is *your* life.

9. Other than thinking you were in love, why did you get married?   (State all reasons, personal and impersonal, no matter how trivial.)

The answers here were similar in all marriages, good and bad: *Sex; wanted children; companionship; because the other person wanted to get married; social acceptance and pressure.*

We're made to feel incomplete if we don't have a partner of the opposite sex. We're bombarded from the day we're born with pro-coupling propaganda. For proof, turn on the television for thirty minutes, pick up a newspaper or magazine and observe. To add to it, as a species, we have natural physical instincts to mate and emotional instincts to proliferate. We're considered abnormal if we want to live alone.

Relatives, friends and acquaintances pressure us. "Haven't you found a husband/wife yet?. I'll never have grandchildren if you don't hurry and get married. If you're not married by the time you're twenty-five, you can forget

37

it All the good ones are gone. You need to find a good man/woman and settle down, have a family. Don't wait around for the fireworks and bells. It just isn't like that."

When others try to control our lives, it's more for their benefit than ours even though they think they're doing it for us. Sometimes our families want brag to their friends about what a great person we married. They're also proud that someone besides them loves us.

If our relationship with another has obviously become sexual, family members in the heartland are still embarrassed. They push us into marriage even though sexual activity or being pregnant is at the top of the list for *worst* reasons to get married. Maybe they're angry because they're humiliated and they unconsciously want to sentence us to life imprisonment. Regardless of the underlying motivation, they certainly want us to hurry and marry so people will quit talking.

Sometimes they're tired of being responsible for us. Not that they *are* responsible, they just feel they are. They want us to have a parent in the accepted form of a spouse since we won't let them parent us anymore.

Apparently, so do we. When we use practical reasons and emotional needs to find a mate, we look for someone who'll treat us pretty much the way our parents did. If our unbalanced parents controlled us with anger, distance or coddling, we pick a mate with similar traits, even to the point of choosing a partner who molests or abuses us if one of our parents did.

We choose a mate who's basic personality traits most closely resemble those of the parent who loved us the least. If neither parent was capable of loving us, our spouse will have the combined traits of both. We're unconsciously trying to recreate a loveless relationship hoping to extract from it the love we never received from the first one. There's more about this later.

10. How well did you get along with your spouse before the marriage?

We generally *get along well* with our potential spouses before we marry, whether we divorce later or not. If we don't get along, we're definitely headed for a bad marriage. Relationships which are bad during courtship *never* improve after the ceremony.

11. List things you have in common with and things that are opposite about you and your spouse.

These answers ranged from *almost everything to almost nothing* with no comparative pattern.

There were happily marrieds who had little in common and unhappily marrieds and divorced who had very much in common with their spouses.

Don't look for someone with whom you have a lot in common and think you'll automatically be happy married to them. And don't think you can't be happy married to someone with whom you have little in common. Either state can be stimulating when lovingly cultivated.

Settling For and Settling Down

12. How soon after the wedding did you encounter real difficulties with your partner?

On the honeymoon to never any real difficulties, with most falling in *the three to six month range*.

Problems great or small surface very soon after the wedding in both good and bad marriages. The differences lie in the three most important bonding foundations for the marriage. In a good marriage spiritual love leads and enlists the reasoning power of the mind and the affection showing abilities of the body. The problems are solved with mutual respect and understanding.

In a bad marriage, one in which the strongest bonds are emotional and physical, we demand fulfillment of selfish needs. Our controlling mind dominates. **I want** (love, affection, reassurance, companionship, sex). **I need** (to be wanted, to compete, to control and feel powerful). **I expect you to give** (compliance). We each reason that we are right and justified in our demands. Problems never get satisfactorily solved.

13. What was the nature of these difficulties?

The happily marrieds, (about 20% overall) if they could come up with a difficulty at all, usually mentioned something trivial like *misunderstandings due to inexperience.*

Unhappily marrieds and divorced mentioned the following: *Drunkenness, neglect, flirtations, dishonesty, unreasonable anger, suspiciousness, jealousy, criticism, money, sexual incompatibility, and others.* These problems were pronounced, though not severe enough to warrant immediate serious action.

14. How did you handle difficulties?

Compensated, appeased, fought, withdrew, ignored, tolerated, surrendered, complied, acquiesced:

> Marrieds: 80%
> Divorced: 100%

Talked about it and decided what to do together:

> Married: 10%
> Divorced: 0%

Said they had no problems:

43

Married: 10%
Divorced: 0%

Early in all marriages normal adjustments to living differently account for some disagreement. Inexperience causes us to handle difficulties poorly.

As you'll see later, those in bad marriages don't improve handling skills with time. Real difficulties come soon and in repeated occasional bursts. They're usually followed by repentance, promises to do better and a period of reconciliation.

Before the next occurrence, we have time to forgive, convince ourselves it won't happen again, and try to forget it. We try not to live in the past or hold a grudge. We take partial blame and resolve to do better ourselves. Or we tell ourselves it's the way things are and we'll just have to live with it if we want to keep the peace.

15. What major or recurring difficulties did (have)

you and your spouse encounter(ed) during the marriage?

At one time or another, all couples disagree over *money, children and/or sex.* They might be recurring disagreements. The determining factor is the *frequency* and *severity* of the disagreement and whether or not a mutually satisfactory solution is agreed upon and implemented.

In bad marriages and all those that ended in divorce there were the *difficulties stated in the answers to question 13, plus laziness, infidelity, lack of communication, indifference, irresponsibility, negativity, raging, moderate violence, embarrassing behavior or appearance, family interference and others.* As in the beginning of the marriage, these problems weren't always extreme, but they were aggravating and frequent enough to be considered problems.

16. How did you deal with them?

It appears a pattern of dealing with problems begins early in a bad marriage and continues without much variation throughout the marriage. The answers here *correspond almost directly with the answers given in question 14* whether counseling was sought or not.

Marriage counseling will only help provided *both* partners are personally balanced and a good counselor can be found. What most people call serious marital problems are usually individual psychological or physiological disorders and would respond better, if at all, to individual treatment.

All counselors should be liberal and experienced enough to realize divorce can sometimes be the best solution, otherwise, their advise will be geared toward making marriage work. Since marriage counseling usually is, controlling spouses often seek it to gain professional support for keeping a bad marriage intact. They follow the direction of the counselor minimally and superficially, very seldom lastingly.

If marriage counseling encourages one-sided appeasement requiring one partner to tolerate or cope, it allows the other to remain stagnant in their behavior. The ideal in marital problem solving is not to satisfy *one*, but to satisfy *both*. We aren't truly accepting our spouses behavior if we feel deprived or repressed. And problems aren't solved if we deny our feelings, we're only pretending they are.

17. How often were (are) you completely satisfied with your partner?

In addition to some "nevers" followed by exclamation points and question marks, percentages ranged from, *"about 10%"* to *"almost always"* with *"75-85%" being most common* among all, married and divorced.

Some low rates of 0-50% came from those married over twenty years. Some high rates 75-85% came from the divorced. I mentioned this question earlier as an example of a poorly worded one.

Notice, divorced persons weren't dissatisfied with their spouses all the time. I've known those who justified staying in a bad marriage by pointing that out, even though their periods of dissatisfaction would be more aptly described as 'hell'.

18. (Married) How do you feel about your spouse now? (Good and Bad)

Most who had been married for more than twenty years, even unhappily, responded with positive feelings such as, *wonderful, good, comfortable, best friend, still enjoy being with them.*

Some added *that they wished their spouses were more 'something' or less 'something'.* Some *had lost some or all respect due to their spouses behavior.*

Some *could barely tolerate them at times.*

Even though about half of these marriages were obviously not good, and I specifically asked for bad feelings, negative answers were few. Sources other than the survey stated the most bad feelings, usually reluctantly, and usually they amply apologized for them.

Negative feelings have always met with disapproval, therefore we usually deny having them. Even if we admit them to ourselves, we carefully avoid expressing them publicly. The next question gives further verification of this fact.

19. (Divorced) How did you feel about your spouse when you were married? (Good and Bad)

The answers here were also positive such as, *thought I loved them, appreciated their good points, felt good about them most of the time.*

So why divorce? Because it isn't that we hate our spouse. We may even like them sometimes. It's that they mean no more to us than most other people we know well. We simply hate being married to them.

And remember too, these respondents have been divorced a while. As you'll see in later answers, ex-spouses don't seem so bad when we don't have to live with them.

There are good times in all marriages. In bad marriages, the good times aren't that great. The bad times are more frequent, more caustic and sustain lasting damage because the healing properties of balanced spiritual love aren't sufficient.

20. (Married) How do you think your spouse feels about you?

70% percent thought *all feelings were mutual.* The other 30% said *they thought their spouses loved them more and stated different reasons for this belief.*

21. (Divorced) How do you think your spouse felt about you when you were married?

Most who divorced their spouses *thought their spouses loved them.* Usually they say they do even when their actions contradict their words. This and other answers about love show that too few of us know what love is.

Some thought their spouses *felt nothing but need.*

22. (Married) When your spouse enters the room or calls you on the telephone, what do you feel upon hearing or seeing them?

The positive answers (about 40%) were, *secure, warm, loved, still thrilled.*

The negative answers (about 20%) were, *tense, irritated, tired.*

40% were brief and inconclusive but similar. Either the

respondents liked surprise phone calls in general or they were surprised when their spouses called. I couldn't determine which. Example: *"It's nice to get a surprise call."* This is clear evidence of our refusal to focus directly on our own feelings, in a word, denial.

23. (Divorced) <u>In the last years</u> **of your marriage, when your spouse entered the room or called you on the telephone, how did you usually feel upon hearing or seeing them?**

All the answers were the same as the negative answers to the preceding question. *Tense, tired, irritated.* There were *no positive answers.*

24. (Married) Which do you feel is the most important reason your spouse remains married to you, love or material and physical need?

Love: 50%

Material, physical and/or emotional need (added by respondents): 30%

All Three: 20%

(Divorced) Which did you feel was the most important reason your spouse remained married to you, love or material or physical need?

Love: 10%

Material, physical and/or emotional need: 60%

All Three: 30%

If so much apparent 'love' in a marriage that ended in divorce seems confusing, look back at the answers to question 21.

25. If material and physical need, how does (did) that make you feel?

Used:

>Married: 0%
>Divorced: 90%

Answers included no personal feelings. Respondents stated opinions about how spouse or all people felt:

>Married: All 30% who thought their spouse remained with them for reasons other than love answered this way.
>Divorced: 10%

When I asked for personal feelings from marrieds, I frequently received answers which contained phrases like, "I think everyone...." and "All marriages...". Again, this is symptomatic of our tendency to avoid facing and analyzing our own feelings. We direct our concentration outward, to our spouses or society as a whole.

Feeling used is demeaning. We don't want to admit our marriage is doing that to us while we're still in it. There's nothing good about being needed; it's only good to be wanted. And as the percentages show, divorced individuals have realized this, confronted their feelings and done something about it.

An arrangement, loosely called a marriage, in which the partners remain in it out of a sense of duty and/or to fulfill material, physical and psychological need is only acceptable if it's acceptable to both partners. It seldom is.

*New opinions are always suspected,
and usually opposed, without any other
reason, but because they are not already
common....*

John Locke..... *An Essay concerning Human
Understanding*

Frig it or Trash it?

It isn't a decision reached in a day. It isn't the result of a fight or a single incident. It evolves. Sometimes a particular event can be sited as the turning point. More often, it's a series of events, slow awakenings, weeks and months of swaying one way or the other, from "I can make it work. I can live with it. I'll just compensate some other way," to "I've got to get out of it. I can't live like this", until "get out of it" is the only option that feels right.

Before we reach that point, it's like driving down

the wrong highway. We tell ourselves and everyone in the car that we're pretty sure we're headed in the right direction. We continue this denial and half-hearted reassurance until we know for sure we must stop and turn around.

26. How many times did (have) you consider(ed) ending the marriage? How many times have (did) you discussed it seriously with your spouse or someone else?

Never.

> Married: 30%
> Divorced: 0%

Only once:

> Married: 10%
> Divorced: 0%

A few to *many* (pun not intended).

> Married: 60%
> Divorced: 100%

If we think about divorce at all, we think about it a lot more than we talk about it. This doesn't mean that if we think about it and talk about it, it will and should happen. The determining factors are the circumstances each time it was considered, the frequency and what resulted.

27. Do (did) you feel your marriage will (would) ever end in divorce? Why or why not?

Married: *No.* 80%

Yes: 10%

Don't know: 10%

Divorced: *No.* 80%

　　　　　Yes: 10%

　　　　　Didn't know: 10%

No misprint. The percentages are the same. We all enter marriage thinking it will last. Even when the trouble begins, we're hopeful we can overcome the difficulties. Good marriages can and do. Parties to a good marriage know it will never end in divorce because they *"still love each other very much.... and never want it to end.."*

In bad or questionable marriages, until we admit it's doomed, we'll *say* we don't *think* it will end in divorce. If we're asked why not, we seldom say we're still in love. We say things like: *"We think divorce is wrong. We made a commitment. The worst is behind us."*

28. How and when did you decide your marriage was bad?

We don't face or admit it right away but we usually

know early in the marriage that it was a mistake.

29. How long was it before you actually did anything about it?

Minimum two years; maximum seventeen years. We live through it until it ends struggling with the wrong spouse, denial and a spirit that demands truth.

30. Why did you wait so long?

Personal Beliefs:

These can be based in religion or not. Some churches prohibit divorce except under certain conditions. If those conditions are not present in our marriage, we feel divorce is wrong. *Right in the Sight of God*, the last section in this book, addresses the religious issue more completely.

Even if we're not religious, our own ethic to finish

what we start, principles, integrity and dedication to commitment urge us to fulfill any vows we make.

Fear of Guilt and Sense of Responsibility:

We hear of sensational divorces that destroy children and drag on in raging battle for months, divorces that were worse than the marriages could possibly have been. Anger and resentment between ex-spouses lasts for years. We don't want to do that to ourselves or our kids. We constantly replay worst case scenarios in our minds. They're even more believable if we're married to a vindictive person.

Fear of Blame:

No matter how much blame we actually deserve for the condition of the marriage, if we're the one who initiates the dissolution, we fear we'll be blamed for the failure of it.

Shame or Pride:

We hate to admit we made a mistake and that

we've been faking for so long. How it will look to everyone else concerns us. We've made most of our social contacts as a married person. We have married friends. We assume that if we want to end our marriage, we'll be scorned, that no one will understand or want to associate with us individually, that they'll feel they must take sides. We avoid even talking about it for fear of being mis-judged no matter what our circumstances are. We feel we must have a reason others will accept as valid, and it has to be a damn good one.

Second bad marriages fall into an either/or category. Either we've learned it's better to get out and we act quickly to end it, or we feel more obligated to make it work since it's even more difficult to admit we goofed twice.

Confusion based on misinformation:

All advice we see or hear about divorce tells us how to "cope" with one. As a result, we think divorce is essentially bad, an ordeal requiring great survival skills. Everyone says it's wrong unless the marriage is horrible.

63

And if the marriage is horrible, the divorce is also classified as horrible. Divorce always gets bad press.

In contrast, all advice on marriage tells how to make it better, implying it must be fundamentally good, worthy of being improved, and that we can improve it if we simply follow a certain formula. Therefore, our minds *reason,* divorce must be much worse than a bad marriage.

Security:

As social animals we have trouble maturing beyond the adolescent years. We need a member of the opposite sex around to validate our sexuality and in case we need an escort. It says to the public we're appealing, we're attractive, we're wanted by someone, no matter what goes on in the privacy of our homes.

We stay in marriages for financial security, afraid of legal expense, afraid we won't be able to manage on a single income.

Emotional instability:

As children, we had certain needs. If they weren't

met by our parents, we continue throughout our lives to seek fulfillment. We marry our parents through our spouses, and since they *are* indeed like our parents, they won't fulfill our needs either.

We didn't learn what to do if our needs were not met. We simply increase demand by trying harder to control. Like infants demanding nourishment, we continually try to persuade our respondents to serve us. In marriage, our respondents are our spouses.

Our needy parents didn't know how to love or leave each other. We didn't know how to leave them. And now, we don't know how to leave any damaging relationship. We hang in there because our parents did and by example pass our twisted, crippled relational skills on to our children and others. This is one of the many damaging things we do by remaining in a bad marriage.

Fear of Being Alone:

We're afraid if we're alone, *none* of our needs will be met. We don't know how to respond to ourselves and fulfill our own needs. We don't know that ultimately we're the only person who will do that dependably. We haven't realized our long list of needs is really a list of *wants* and should never be treated as anything more. All we really *need* is air, water and food.

Low expectations:

When we marry, we hope ours will be one of the good ones. But when it isn't, we're not surprised. We know most marriages aren't good, so we settle for what we get.

Apathy:

When we suppress our feelings we suppress our drive, our emotional energy to change and grow. We excuse our oppression induced laziness by telling ourselves we've waited too long, that we can live with it, that divorce is wrong and too much trouble, that being out wouldn't be much better than being in.

For years, our minds can keep our spirits in retreat. We're programmed to believe our relationships with everyone, including God, and even our material possessions are all glued together with our marriage. If our marriage fails, our lives will fall into an un-mendable heap of ruin. That's just one more ridiculous lie.

We can be a mother or father or friend whether we're married or not. We're sons or daughters, sisters or brothers, religious or atheist whether or not we're husbands and wives. Those things don't change when our marital status changes.

Logically, whatever we are, we'll be better if we aren't in the emotional turmoil a bad marriage produces. We can't become balanced as individuals unless we detach ourselves from damaging relationships. What we become may very well depend on whether or not we know when to walk away.

31. Were both parties agreeable to the divorce?

Almost all met with initial argument.

We fear opposition. We expect anger, emotional upheaval, retaliation and negativity because we've lived with it for years. We've spent years learning not to cause it. Telling our spouse we plan to divorce them begins the end of worrying about it.

32. If not, what were the reasons given by the opposing party?

The responses were the same from all opposers, they stated the reasons we've always heard, *children, family, finances, responsibility, religion. We hear the usual promises to reform. We hear how we're no better than they are, implying we deserve them, as though that's reason enough to stay married.*

In many unbalanced relationships a sadomasochistic, persecutor/victim pattern is established. Before you picture perverts, chains and whips, let me bring it a little closer to home.

Sadism is a delight in cruelty, pleasure from someone else's mental or physical pain derived by

inflicting or observing abuse. To abuse is to damage or injure by word or action. That broadens the scope considerably, doesn't it?

Of course, no one seriously admits they're sadistic. But sadists are the people who gather at a fire, an execution, a fight, commercially staged or not, and the scene of a horrible accident. They are the people who give icky details when they describe illnesses, surgery and death, and they do love to describe them. Because of sadists and masochists, violence, disaster and suffering are popular sports and media fare. Sadomasochism of different degrees is a common human condition.

Masochism is pleasure in being dominated or abused physically or mentally. No one admits they take pleasure in this either, yet we endure abuse and dominance for long periods of time and do nothing to change it. Sadomasochists deliberately provoke both responses. One partner can be unknowingly caught in this sick pattern simply because they're married to a sadomasochist. The cycle goes like this:

The *sadist/persecutor* is irritable, angry, critical,

69

withdrawn and disagreeable. If they site reasons for their behavior, the reasons are vague or exaggerated. The *masochist/victim* reacts and begins the cycle by being *good, compliant,* patient and understanding in an attempt to alter the persecutors state of mind. Nothing works. Persecutors continue, sometimes for months, until they achieve their alternate purpose, which is to be punished or abused themselves.

The original victim eventually reaches a breaking point and, even if divorce is never mentioned, the persecutor gets the message. The victim won't take anymore. They're fed up and angry themselves. They strike back defensively. Although this is a normal reaction, the sadomasochist sees it as the punishment they wanted. The unwilling victim then becomes the unwilling persecutor. The original persecutor immediately assumes the role of victim, the one suffering, the one being dominated. They become *good, complying* to every whim of their persecutor until desired reconciliation is achieved.

The peak of the reconciliation period is relatively

calm. The sadomasochist is waiting to regain dominance and the unwilling partner simply believes things are better. It can last for months, until the sadomasochist feels secure or powerful enough to assume the persecutor role again and the desire to dominate returns.

If one has a predominately sadistic disorder, they won't be quite so good during the victim stage and it will last only long enough for the partner to quit 'persecuting'. If this doesn't happen in the time the sadist thinks it should, they'll probably react with more cruelty. If one is predominately masochistic, they'll create conditions under which they'll be victimized. They're terminal doormats. Look around you. Many people and relationships exhibit these characteristics with different levels of severity.

Surprisingly, even when one is unwilling, both parties to such a relationship are controllers who wish to dominate. We all know there are pleas-ers and pleas-ees. In reality, there are merely compliant masochists (pleasers) and dominate sadists (pleas-ees).

Pleasers try to control response by being good. It's the same principal under which we expect a friendly greeting in return for ours, the "I'm nice to you; you should be nice to me" syndrome. Pleasers expect a reasonable amount of reciprocal compliance, affection, respect and glory in exchange for their goodness.

Pleas-ees try to control response by demand. It's the, "I want it and I want it now!" principle. They have temper tantrums, ailments and problems. They plead, pout, whine, threaten and complain. They're helpless and needy.

Most people are a combination of both. Whatever we do, whether demanding or complying, if we do it hoping to provoke response or reaction from someone else, we're doing it to control them. The desire to control comes from our egotistical, needy mind. It doesn't matter so much why we're this way; it matters more that we realize we are.

The sicker the mind, the stronger the desire to sustain a relationship at all costs. These people don't care *why* their partners remain with them. They don't care if their partners are unhappy. They just want them to stay. They create as many binders as they can - children, family ties, guilt, fear, chronic psychosomatic illnesses, financial difficulties and forced dependency, like giving up driving (for contrived reasons) so they'll have to be driven everywhere. They dominate and beg to be dominated. The demands increase at the same time they're promising to do anything to make the marriage better.

To truly make things better, everyone should dominate themselves and take control of their own life whether they're married or not. If self-improvement is made conditional upon a marriage remaining intact, it's fakery, just one more attempt to control.

In contrast, if our partner agrees to a divorce too quickly, as they sometimes do, *we* might feel a bit rejected. But did we really want out of the marriage or were we trying to provoke the reform and reconciliation response? If the later, we should acknowledge our own desire to control others and work toward changing ourselves.

33. How did the initiating party handle the objections.

Ignored them. Stood firm.

This was the only answer given. It's the only sensible thing to do. Anything else is a waste of time and emotional energy. When we don't react predictably to attempts to persuade us to change our mind, the opposition ceases. It doesn't always cease immediately, but it does cease. It takes two people to argue.

Look at the next question for a healthy response to a request for divorce.

34. (Married) If your spouse told you they wanted a divorce, what would you think and do?

About 50% *said they would let their spouses go.*

About 40% said *they would be angry or try harder to make their spouses happy.*

About 10% obviously didn't take the question seriously.

Upon being asked for a divorce, the parties in the first answer would realize they had done their best and it wasn't good enough, that their spouses believe they would be happier without them. *Some* had trouble imagining my scenario, but said that even though they would be heartbroken, they would respect the wishes of their spouse and let them go. This is love.

Spiritually loving, balanced people do not want to stay married to someone who doesn't want to be married to them. They neither attempt to *control* their spouses nor stand in the way of their happiness.

At first look, the last part of the second answer may seem positive, as though it should be included in the first answer. It isn't and it shouldn't. Both parts of the second answer are controlling reactions.

35. If you told your spouse you wanted a divorce, what do you think your spouse would think and do?

Except for those in the worst marriages, most respondents *expected reactions from their spouses similar to their own.*

"The child becomes the focus of the relationship.....
Actually the identified patient (emotionally
disturbed child) is only a symptom of the
emotionally disturbed marriage."

John Bradshaw from
Bradshaw on: The Family

Somebody's Gonna Get Hurt!

A judge finds before him a couple in their nineties suing for divorce.
He asks the woman, "Are you sure this is what you want?"
"I hate the bastard," she replies.
The judge turns to the man, "And you. How do you feel?"
"Another day with her is another day in Hell," he says.
The judge studies them a moment. "But your ages..... Why did you wait so long?"
"We had to wait for the children to die," the woman answers.

Children, other family members and friends play a vital role in our decision to stay in or get out of a marriage. We hear mostly about the troubled children, the ones who don't adjust. We're bombarded with classificatory phrases like "Broken Homes" and "Children of Divorce" always spoken or written in disapproving context. But homes can be broken without a divorce. And problem children are never products of divorce.

Small children, the elderly and invalids should be carefully planned for if they're truly dependent on us. But we don't have to, and we shouldn't suffer in a bad marriage for their sake.

We are *not responsible* for other adults, either spouses or grown children. If we think we are, we have the savior complex. How important we are, how powerful, how superior, how heroic, how egotistical. We think by sacrificing ourselves to a bad marriage, we control the quality of life for another mentally, physically functional adult.

In the case of spouses, we think they can't think for themselves, master a new task, adjust to change, manage their business, make decisions or take care of themselves.

In the case of adult children, we're so insecure we

don't think they'll love us if we divorce their mother or father. Like our spouses, if they want our sacrifice to continue, they'll tell us the same thing. Or it could be that we only relate to our children through our spouse and we fear the responsibility of direct contact. There'll be no more "your father says" or "talk to your mother about it". If anything goes wrong there's no one to whom we can divert blame.

Hurting the children and family is an area in which potential problems are so extremely exaggerated and *misclassified* that we fear taking the chance. We make our decision to end a marriage laboriously never realizing how right it is until we do it and see the results.

36. When you told your children, how did they react to your decision?

Younger children: (less than eight years of age), *initial apprehension, confusion, resistance.*

Older children: *Understanding mostly, some apprehension.*

Good People... Bad Marriages

This is the position at which our determination is tested the most. At first mention of divorce, young children are going to be shaken. It's unrealistic to expect anything else. Although their optimally functioning spirits allow them to adapt quickly to change if adults take charge, they're leery of unknown territory.

Just try telling a five year old the family's moving to Kissimee. You'll get the quickest 'uh-uh-not-me-buddy' expression you've ever seen unless they know that's where Disneyworld is.

They're even less informed about divorce than we are. All they know about it is, both parents don't live in the same house. If it frightened us to think about it, what do you think it'll do to them?

If we're the non-custodial parent, physically we'll be with our children more if we remain married. But we're usually so tense and preoccupied we hardly know they're there. Children feel the tension as much or more than we do. If we're enduring all this tension to be with them, 'for them', as we say, that makes them *responsible for keeping us in it.*

Sometimes we become too involved in their lives by overly dominating them or imposing ourselves into their activities to compensate for deficiencies in ourselves or the marital relationship. In doing so, we also make them *responsible for our happiness.*

They don't consciously know they have these responsibilities, so how can they tell us they don't want them? They try to do the job we've assigned them and they're not qualified. They try to divert attention from our problems by being generally problematic themselves. They may be rebellious, overachievers, underachievers, overly controlled or controlling, overly competitive, accident prone, given to physical or emotional complaints, eating disorders or addictions. They may cling to their parents, even through adulthood, not to fill their own needs, but to fill the needs of the parents.

They're the bonding agent for the marriage. If it falls apart and they were holding it together, they'll feel they failed. Responsibility for a bad marriage is fraught with guilt, confusion and fear. No one wants to do that to a child.

They have keenly developed demand and response intelligence. Our biggest weakness is a desire to respond to their needs and they know it. Out of fear of the unknown and because of the responsibility we've given them, they may do everything in their power to see that things remain the same. Don't continue to make them responsible by letting them talk you out of it.

If we take responsibility, as we should, deal with the problem and make it plain to the children that the decision to stay in it or end it has nothing to do with them, they'll be unconsciously relieved. Like the garbage we generate by lazy selfishness, we should scrupulously dispose of a bad marriage without dumping it in our children's world.

When you tell them the marriage is ending, listen to how they feel. Assure them you're concerned with how it will affect them, but not to the point you're willing to change your mind. This may sound harsh, but it takes the burden off them and puts it with the parent where it belongs. They'll adjust more quickly if they aren't wondering if they can do something about it.

Sometimes an unbalanced parent will attempt to enlist the aid of the child in keeping the marriage together by invoking sympathy for themselves or asking advice from the children. If it happens, tell the child why the other parent acted this way, that it was wrong and let it go at that.

John Bradshaw has written several good books on what dysfunctional relationships are and the damage incurred by their sustenance. His books are invaluable tools for achieving individual wholeness, a necessary condition in a marriage or out.

As much as it is in your power, don't change too much about your children's lives, i.e. schools, neighborhoods, living conditions. Tell them calmly what they can expect. Where they'll live, how often they'll see their other parent, how much their lives will or won't change. You shouldn't talk to them until you have most of the answers.

It's important to separate the marriage from the parent-child relationship, both for you and the children. Don't detail your marital problems and don't tell them how your spouse is going to treat them. Tell them not to be afraid to talk about how they feel, and make sure they have no reason to be. Talk to them as long and as often as necessary.

Without expressing bitterness and cynicism, tell them how you feel, i.e. "Our marriage was a mistake. I'm not happy. I haven't been for a long time. I'm tense and tired and I can't be a good person or a good parent feeling like that." Don't tell them how they should feel or how your spouse feels. You can only speak for yourself.

Adolescent children will probably understand, although they may object to a potential change in lifestyle. Like us, they worry about telling their friends. Their fears are ungrounded. Their peers are going to give it even less attention than ours. Unlike Charles' and Di's, your divorce isn't going to be a hot topic for months, weeks or even days. People have their own lives to live. Your life isn't going to hold their attention for more than a few minutes even if you want it to.

Some adolescent and grown children may be firmly planted in the role of responsibility and object initially simply because they think they should. But they know the marriage wasn't good. They were eye witnesses.

37. One year later, how were they doing? Two years later?

I combined these questions because most children were completely adjusted to their parents being apart in less than one year. The following responses included children of all ages:

> *"My grown children were glad for me."*
>
> *"It took my teenage daughter a few weeks to adjust to a new lifestyle. Now she loves it. She's changed completely. She's outgoing, relaxed and assertive. Before she was burdened, fearful, clingy and paranoid."*
>
> *"After the divorce I was able to concentrate on my relationship with my children. They were happier. They felt I loved them more."*
>
> *"My children didn't unanimously support my*

decision to begin with, especially the younger ones. But by the end of two years they understood completely."

    "My kids and I are happier than we've ever been."

If children are still having problems adjusting a year after the divorce or you feel your relationship with them has taken a turn for the worse, the divorce isn't the problem. It simply gets the blame. Children are more likely damaged by a lengthy bad marriage or the emotional instability of one or both parents.

Don't allow them or your spouse to use either the marriage or the divorce as an excuse for anti-social behavior. We've all suffered damage. It isn't just a matter of some people reacting differently. It's a matter of explaining, excusing and allowing it to continue because we feel guilty. Don't be manipulated. Individual counseling is available.

If your children are unhappy or they don't want to be with you, before you ask them why, ask yourself why. Are you using your child against your ex-spouse as a spy, a battering ram, a beggar or a basher? Are you using them to insinuate yourself into your ex-spouse's life? What do you do and say when you're around them? Do you whine, complain and feel sorry for yourself?

Are you interested in their life or are they having to tolerate yours? Is your behavior causing them to lose respect for you? Are you flouting immoral or anti-social behavior? Do you do things in front of them you wouldn't allow them to do?

Are you deciding what you'll do with them or are you asking them what they'd like to do? Are you trying to make them happy or are they having to make you happy? Don't lie to yourself. What goes on after the divorce, went on before the divorce. It's just as damaging either way.

You may encounter some problems as a result of human nature, especially the nature of children. You simply have to avoid behaving on or below their maturity level. Don't compete in any way with your ex-spouse.

You may hear things like, "Daddy's giving me three hundred dollars for my birthday." ("Can you top that?" is only implied.) You could run and make out a check for four hundred dollars and hope it doesn't bounce or you can be glad he gave three hundred dollars and you won't have to give so much. They'll love you more for a thoughtful gift than for an expensive one.

Don't be a time keeper. Don't insist they alter their plans to fit your schedule or the court's schedule. Court commands are a safety net in case one party isn't cooperative. If both spouses cooperated with the children's welfare as their *only* motivation, court decrees wouldn't be needed. If everybody's happy, the courts aren't going to know or care what you're doing.

Everybody can be happy. Keep the communication lines and your mind open. Be flexible, positive and discreet. (By the way, discreet means showing good judgement in action and speech. It doesn't mean being secretive.) Spend as much time with your children as you can, but make sure it's helping them, not hurting them. If you do this, you won't likely get opposition from your ex or anyone else.

38. How did others who were directly affected by the divorce react to the announcement? (i.e. dependents or

semi-dependents, related or not.) One year later, how were they adjusting? Two years later?

"Supported me completely. Wondered why it took me so long. Wondered what would happen to them." Almost unanimous.

In some cases, when we've been married for many years, there are others who are our dependents or semi-dependents. They might be foster children, parents or invalid relatives. They may live with us or we may provide for them in other ways.

Think about what can be done, discuss it with your attorney and your spouse, if practicable, and come up with a plan that will be agreeable to all concerned. Then when you tell the affected party of your decision, you'll have some options that will relieve their worries.

Listen to their concerns and suggestions, be open to their input but, as with the children, don't let worry for them change your mind. Odds are, they've felt the tension in your marriage and will be relieved it's coming to an end.

Much like the children they may be apprehensive about change but they'll adjust readily, long before one year has passed.

40. How did you feel about telling others your marriage was over?

Uncomfortable. Afraid they would disapprove. Guilty. Ashamed. Most of the divorced respondents gave one or all of these answers.

Think about someone you love, a child, a parent, a brother, sister or friend telling you they had decided to end their marriage. You wouldn't want them to have the feelings portrayed in those answers. And neither do those who love you.

39. What kind of encouragement or discouragement concerning the divorce did you receive from other people?

Again, almost unanimous *support*.

Only a few *negative responses came from parents-in-law*.

Even fewer *parents, siblings or friends dutifully encouraged working at it*.

This is one of the reactions we fear the most and we shouldn't fear it at all. Our friends and family know us. They know we don't make decisions on a whim, that we've tried our best. And they know we've had a lousy marriage. They may be surprised we're actually doing something about it, but that isn't disapproval.

If in-laws disapprove, don't be too surprised. Parents are protective of their children and to them, divorce, when not initiated by their children, is synonymous with rejection, persecution and desertion.

91

Disapproval from anyone is partially a self-defensive response. Unbalanced people are extremely protective of their own established relational methods however warped they may be. If they admit you're right to get out, they have to admit they're wrong to stay in. They retaliate by trying to make you feel more guilty so they'll feel less guilty.

Just because someone is related to you or has proclaimed themselves to be your friend doesn't mean they're capable of truly loving you. Those who love you want you to be happy; the rest don't matter.

40. How did the reactions of other people affect you?

I felt comforted, relieved, encouraged, like I was doing the right thing.

How quickly others adjust immediately following the divorce depends on us a great deal. There are no written rules of etiquette for divorced persons that I'm aware of. Showing consideration works well whatever the circumstances.

Until tensions ease, make sure in a nice way that your ex won't be where you're going to be at the same time. Call first, but don't say, "She's not coming is she? If she is, count me out." Say something like, "Right now, I'd feel uncomfortable being there at the same time as _____, I'd love to come before or after though."

For a while, you may want to avoid situations which might be uncomfortable for you, such as holiday gatherings and functions which would normally have been attended by both you and your spouse. If you have children, make sure get togethers with them aren't taxed with accidental meetings and uninvited guests in the form of dates.

If you're dating, ask your family and friends how they feel about having your date attend the function with you. Chances are good, they won't mind. But in the beginning, some of them, usually children or parents, may not be comfortable accepting someone else in the place of your spouse. If they ask you not to bring a date, respect their wishes and don't make a big deal out of it. You can go other places with your date. If your new relationship is serious, acceptance will come more quickly and with less resentment if it isn't forced.

Until the bitterness subsides, there'll be a strong temptation to tell everyone what a loser you married. Our purpose in spouse bashing is mostly to get sympathy, divert blame or keep others from trying to talk us into reconciliation.

You'll have to contend with surprisingly little unwanted advice, so don't bash 'just in case.' And don't bash if it does happen. Simply repeat these lines. "It was a mistake. We weren't good for each other. I've thought about it a long time. It's best for everyone. I appreciate your concern, but I'd rather not talk about it."

If friends and relatives bash for you, don't encourage it. If they're unjust in their bashes, speak up, then change the subject.

THE ATTORNEY, MY EX AND I

41. Who initiated the final dissolution and how did they do it?

The majority of my sources *initiated the divorce action.* Some *saw an attorney first,* which is the best way to proceed if conditions allow it.

You can talk to an attorney without filing for divorce. The first visit is usually for informational purposes. They can advise you of your rights, what to expect in the way of a settlement and what you should or shouldn't do to avoid legally jeopardizing your position.

Some respondents *moved out first, then saw an attorney.* Some *confronted their spouse* with their decision first. There's no right way and no wrong way. We each have to do it our way, according to our situation.

It's the first turning step and surprisingly easy. Those few unsteady minutes will begin your trip to freedom. A trip that will seem short compared to time spent in a bad marriage.

If you have much property or can't agree on some point, it will take more time. Attorneys aren't famous for speed. Different states have different laws. Your attorney can explain everything. That's one of the few things they do quickly.

To find the right attorney, take your time. The best way is to ask people you know. Get the names of several if you can. Base your choice on professional performance alone. You don't have to say why you need one if you're uncomfortable doing so. Just say you have some legal questions about getting your future in order.

Some Telephone listings show the services offered

by a legal firm. If not, call the attorney's office and ask if they handle divorces. If they don't, ask them to recommend someone who does. Good attorneys know other good attorneys. Some offer a free first consultation. Ask about fees when you call.

The attorney will question you about your reasons for wanting a divorce. Although they may seem to be grilling you, they aren't disapproving or trying to change your mind. If you feel they are, change attorneys. What they should be doing is determining how serious you are and what they've got to work with should a court battle ensue.

Some states, counties or cities offer legal aid to those with low incomes. Call Social Services (not Social Security) or Human Services listed under the government listings in the phone book. A general information number usually begins all government listings. Call that, if you can't find a number, and tell them what you need.

The YMCA and YWCA have services (not legal) for low income individuals who want to improve their career potential. Call and ask what they offer. Depending on who answers the phone, they also may be able to recommend a good attorney. Organizations for battered women may give you some names, but don't count on it. Ask the librarian. Think. Be creative and resourceful.

Property isn't an important factor when we reach the limit of our tolerance. It's a thing, touchable, destructible, replaceable, jointly owned by legal documentation. As a rule, property, or the value thereof, which was accumulated during the marriage is divided equally regardless of earnings.

To get an idea of how that happens, make a list of everything the two of you own, from the lawn mower to the house. It may take several days to remember it all and you'll still leave something off. That's normal. Don't worry about it. The attorney will ask about the big things, so what you don't remember probably doesn't really matter. Make one column for things you want, and another for things you think your spouse will want.

Estimate the fair market value of each item. That's approximately what it's worth now, not what you paid for it. You're wasting time if you fudge prices to make it

98

come out the way you want. If you need help determining value, talk to a dealer, i.e. used household goods, jewelry, auto, real estate.

Remember, parcels of real estate can be divided and exchanged for value if they're large enough. All it takes is a survey and a new deed. Add savings, retirement accounts, other cash, etc. and total both columns. These are your assets.

Next, make a list of all your debts, present unpaid balances on credit cards, auto loans, home mortgages, etc., (not monthly bills). These are your liabilities. Subtract your liabilities from your assets. This figure will be your joint net worth.

Your column total should approximately equal your spouses column total. If it doesn't, and the difference is significant, some shifting of liabilities or assets will be necessary. Always add assets and subtract liabilities.

If you hear of a long legal battle over property, someone is probably trying to get more than their share or using property as a means of control or revenge. Don't be bullied into compliance by threats of a court battle. The courts will be fair. Fair is good enough when we really want out. Don't use property division as an excuse for apathy. Material possessions are part of the structure that imprisons us in a bad marriage. Freedom is priceless.

There are federal laws that mandate child support amounts based on the number of children and a percentage of the non-custodial parents income. Arguments over this issue have been abolished. There are stiff laws governing nonpayment. This was not a noted problem with my sources.

There were no specific questions about finances on the survey. They were mentioned as marital difficulties but not as divorce or post-divorce problems.

While in a bad marriage, we tend to spend foolishly in an attempt to buy happiness. We try to console ourselves with things. Women redecorate and buy cosmetics, clothes and jewelry. Men buy tools and recreational equipment. We remodel the house instead of our lives and buy cars so we'll have financial excuses to go nowhere.

Unless we're presently homeless, we could all

probably live on a lot less. Explore your options before you say it can't be done. Decide how much you're willing to pay for contentment. Making ends meet can be a challenging adventure instead of a chore.

In most cases, if we take a hard look, we'll see that we can live well even if we're single. Financial Self-Defense by Charles J. Givens is an excellent book on living on less. There are a number of others. Ask your librarian or book store clerk.

42. What problems, if any, did you encounter legally?

None and almost none were the answers here. Only a few mentioned *slow attorneys and slow spousal response to necessary signatures.*

Usually the parties in a bad marriage have been unhappy so long, they want the contention to end along with the marriage. Often they agree on all points before they actually have the papers drawn up. It's not uncommon for one attorney to do everything.

101

A word of caution: If you didn't trust your spouse during the marriage, don't trust them during the divorce. If distrust is the norm, I strongly recommend separate attorneys.

43. What problems, if any, did you encounter emotionally?

Almost none was the most common answer. Some (less than 25%) expressed *a sense of loss* for different reasons.

When life changes, we must adjust. There's always a down side to adjustment. To gain something, we always lose something. The same is true if we marry, change jobs, move to another city, have a child, if children leave home, if we retire, if illness strikes, after a death. I could go on and on. If you're living, your life will change.

Adjusting to the change brought about when we end a bad marriage is a relatively easy when compared to the marriage. All sources agreed. Even if we do feel a certain amount of loss or disorientation initially, any

102

negative feelings we have weigh poorly against the uplifting relief, peace, and freedom we gain.

44. How did you cope with these problems?

Work, hobbies and increased social activity were the most popular ways of getting through the transitional period.

45. Once you knew the marriage was over, how did you feel? (Include both positive and negative feelings.)

The most frequent positive feeling was *relief.*

We don't realize the constant level of tension we've been living with until we're relieved of it. Bad marriages don't reveal themselves suddenly. They build over a period of years. We condition ourselves to carry the weight gradually.

The most frequent negative feeling was *a sense of failure.*

We all want to succeed, especially at marriage. But bad marriages are bound to fail no matter what we do to prevent it. We unknowingly start with incompatible mixes. It's like cooking and substituting the wrong ingredients or trying to run a diesel engine on gasoline.

Keeping a marriage license valid and living in the same house doesn't mean the marriage hasn't failed. And if our marriage fails, it doesn't mean we failed. Longevity in a marriage is no indicator of quality or success. A bad marriage can last just as long as a good one.

46. Concerning the divorce, how did the difficulties you actually encountered compare with the difficulties you had imagined you would encounter?

It was much easier than I thought it would be was the most common answer.

The divorce process progresses with about the same or less difficulty than the marriage did, never more. This could be attributable mainly to these two things:

(1.) A spouse who hopes to continue the established sadomasochistic pattern of revolt and reconciliation, victim and persecutor will be in the being-punished-being-good-needy-victim-hoping-for-reconciliation mode and therefore on good behavior most of the time.

(2.) A more balanced spouse, or one who simply wants out, will be agreeable.

How much difficulty you encounter during the weeks surrounding the divorce is largely dependent on your ability to adjust to change, your mental stability and that of your marriage partner. Unless they're truly psychotic, even the most vindictive spouse loses interest in revenge in a matter of months.

Special Note: I received surveys from persons whose spouses severely abused them physically. I felt the conditions in their marriages were too atrocious to be included in my study, but I mention them here to make a point

They all encountered difficulties during the

divorce, even when the spouse was originally agreeable to it. They and their children had emotional difficulties up to and beyond two years following the divorce. They all blamed the divorce like most people do. The divorce was obviously no worse than the marriage. By saying the divorce was the cause of the difficulties during it and following it, they're implying things would have been better if they hadn't divorced. Contradictorily, they all said their lives were much better since the divorce.

My point? Don't blame the divorce for problems the marriage created or for damage caused by the personality disorders of the parents. The divorce was part of the solution. It's time to give it the credit it's due.

Did We Learn Anything?

47. (Married) If you had it to do over, would you marry the same person?

Yes. 70%
No: 20%
Not sure: 10%

48. (Divorced) From courtship to marriage, if you had it to do over, what would you do differently?

Almost all *said they would be more careful about whom they married or not get married at all, and certainly not marry the same person.* Only one *said they had no real regrets.*

49. (Married) Do you think you would have been as satisfied with someone else? If yes, explain your answer.

Yes: 60%
No: 30%
Undecided: 10%

Those who said yes usually reasoned someone else could have been chosen with the same or better 'qualifications' than the person they married.

50. (Divorced) How do you feel about your life now as opposed to your life when you were married.

"Then I crawled. Now I fly." This was the best

summation of the most common answer: (95%)

Are we lonely and depressed? Do we get discouraged? Are we unsure and insecure? *Sometimes.* But not nearly as often as when we were married.

51. How do you feel about your former spouse now compared to how you felt about them when you were married to them?

About the same. Only now I don't have to cope with them or try to love them. The less I have to do with them, the less I think about them. This represents the majority.

Finally admitting to ourselves that we dislike our spouse, or don't like them well enough to be married to them is difficult. It takes complete honesty. It means reversal of denial and goes against our lifelong conditioning. It also marks the end of the tragic play we call a marriage whether a legal divorce follows immediately or not.

During the marriage, we're busy in our roles, taking our cues and trying to force ourselves to feel something we don't. We must make our act convincing, not only to others, but to ourselves. We won't think about what we really feel, only what we *should* feel. Giving up the pressure of performing accounts for some of the relief we feel after a divorce.

We may encounter some trying times with our spouse during the break-up, but no more than we frequently encountered during our marriage. We may encounter some trying times in the post divorce weeks while we both adjust to the change. Sometimes tension lasts up to a year, seldom longer, and progresses in a steadily diminishing pattern.

For those coming out of really awful marriages or those who are struggling with instability, bitterness lasts longer, two or three years. But it does abate. Those people we sometimes thought we hated, don't look so bad when we don't have to look at them very often.

In most cases, when tension levels off, the relationship becomes something like casual friendship. If we think of them at all, we think of them as individuals, not as our husband or wife. They become much more tolerable. The friendship isn't deep. No physical attraction remains. We're acquaintances. That's probably all we should have been.

52. How do you feel about remarriage?

Most *said they were neither opposed to it nor desirous of it.*

53. If you aren't opposed to remarriage, what would be your criteria for choosing your next spouse?

100% need-based answers, what-can-you-do-for-me qualifications. No mention of love.

If we jump into another marriage for practical reasons, we'll have the same disastrous results. We may use different criteria for the second spouse, but they still come from our needy minds. Our minds obviously cannot formulate a good marriage.

We should wait, become whole and balanced ourselves, learn to be satisfied with our individuality, not force, not rush, and let our spirits lead us. When and if the time is right and the person is right, we'll know without a doubt.

54. If someone told you they weren't happy in their marriage, what would you say to them?

The most common answers were disappointing but not surprising.

Work at it; All marriages require work; If your partner isn't a really bad person, you should try to love them; No marriage is "happy" all the time; You made a commitment; Don't give up and quit; Get counseling.

Married: 80%
Divorced (mostly counseling): 25%

I'd try to help them define the problems and their feelings.

Married: 20%
Divorced: 10%

Don't wait. Get out.

Married: 0%
Divorced: 65%

The fewest and best answers (only 10% overall) were completely non-judgmental. The respondents said in essence, *"I'd listen but offer no advice. **I think we all know how to solve our own problems; we just may not have faced what we'll have to do."***

How quickly we advise. How readily we think someone wants us to solve their problems. How easy it seems to straighten out everybody else's life. It's no wonder nobody talks. No matter what our training or experience, we don't have the skills or knowledge to judge whether or not a marriage is worth saving unless it's our own.

Obviously, partners in a marriage which lasts more than a couple of years aren't flighty and casual about their commitment. A good number of people seem to think they are. Does that misjudgment come from ignorance, thoughtlessness or both?

People in good marriages say 'work at it' because they put a little loving effort into their marriage and get nice results. They share and improve. They have no real concept of bad marriages and should never presume to advise. What works for a basically good marriage clearly will not work for a basically bad one.

The rest say 'work at it' because everybody says 'work at it'. Usually they're unhappily slaving away at it themselves. They too, should never advise. If a marriage has lasted for years, the partners have already worked at it. It isn't working. By repeating 'work at it' we imply they simply haven't worked hard enough. Hard work won't make a bad marriage better.

Trying to make a marriage work without love is

like building a house on soft ground without a proper foundation. You'll work for years constantly trying to prevent your house from falling. At any point you can admit you made a mistake and move out. Or you can keep working until you're exhausted, let it fall and live in the rubble until you die.

Legal divorce isn't the failure of a marriage. It only makes it public. The marriage was never anything other than a failure. No formula for improvement applies.

55. In your estimation, what percentage of all marriages are as good as yours?

20% *was most popular.* 10-15% *was next but not close.* A few said *less than 10%.*

The general interpretation of this question was "what percentage of all marriages are good?" It should have been stated that way. Some said they didn't know anyone who had a good marriage and that, sadly, would include their own. Since there are too few good marriages, we compare ours to other bad ones and it looks about average.

Would we buy stock with only a twenty percent chance of gaining an income from it? Yes, if there was pressure to invest and that was the best investment available. Would we take a job if there was a eighty-five percent chance we would be miserable in it? Yes, if most jobs had the same potential. Would we buy a car if we knew it was mechanically unsound. Yes, if eighty per cent of all cars were mechanically unsound.

Mind guided people like to control. When they form majority attitude they become 'society'. As a society, we're afraid if we give divorce a positive image that people will take the marital commitment too lightly, that they'll want out at the least provocation. This just isn't true.

Society has panicked in the face of a mounting divorce rate and is pushing "Good Old Fashioned Family Values," with subliminal messages that tell us this means lasting marriages and children produced by that marriage. People want to conform to what society expects, therefore they pretend they have an old fashioned family with values when what they really have is a facade. What we should push is values in general. Self-value or self-respect should be taught in schools.

People who value themselves don't feel compelled to find a member of the opposite sex to validate their self-worth. And they wouldn't feel the need to pretend they had when it became obvious that they hadn't.

Commitment comes from the heart. Partners in the best marriages remain there because they both want to, not because either of them feels they have to. The only thing society does by dictating that marriage is right and divorce is wrong, is to compel people to stay in a marriage when heartfelt commitment, for whatever reason, is absent in one or both partners.

It's impossible to influence people to end a good marriage. And unfortunately for those in one, it's usually impossible to influence a bad marriage into dissolution. Society cannot alter personal feelings by force feeding its ideals. All it does is cause conflict in individuals, a battle between what we really feel and what society tells us we should or shouldn't do.

Society becomes a controller who manipulates by producing guilt. Guilt only works against those who have a conscience and those would be the same ones who take commitment seriously to begin with. The recipients of the control don't need it. The rest ignore it. Therefore, it's only harmful.

Society's efforts would be better directed toward showing us how to make both right, either marriage or divorce. The choice should be ours. The end result of such reconcentration of imposed ideals would be lasting marriages that are good and practical divorces that are also good.

Marital partners might be more conscious of their behavior if they knew society wouldn't encourage tolerance by attempting to keep all marriages intact. Those who make unsatisfactory partners for any marriage probably wouldn't be married at all, or at worst, married to someone with equal imbalance.

Relationships should never be sustained because of a sense of obligation. If they are, they become a burden.

All the parties involved feel the weight. To a person whose spirit is strong enough to rebel, the weight is tremendous.

Having a good marriage is wonderful. Having no marriage instead of a bad marriage is also wonderful. It's important that we accept that premise. Consider the following circumstance. This could be someone you know:

"At night and weekends, if I'm not busy with one of my other hobbies, I read, listen to music or watch something on television. Sometimes I go for a walk or take a long leisurely bath. My days are filled with the usual irritations but I know at the end of them I'll be at home away from the pressure. I can totally relax there. It makes everything seem less important, easier to tolerate.

If I'm lonely or want to discuss an issue, I call a friend. Sometimes friends call me. They might be male or female. I can talk on the phone as long as I like. Sometimes we go out or I invite them over. They can stay as long as we both please.

I can develop a relationship or end it but I don't feel pressured to have one. I can live frugally and refuse to let my career dominate my life or I can throw myself into my job and work eighty hours a week. I can blow my savings or eat rice for a week and heat one room to save money.

I can do whatever I want, whenever I want, with whomever I choose. I'm not afraid to make decisions. I take responsibility. I take credit. I take blame. There's always someone to call when I need something. I have problems, good luck, bad luck, good days and bad days.

I'm not a bad person. My parents, children and friends love me. More importantly, I love me. Age will eventually overtake me. Then I'll have few diversions except interesting memories. But I have friends of all ages. My children will still enjoy being with me. They tell me I'm open, interesting and enthusiastic, truly "young at heart", a positive and valuable influence.

I wasn't afraid to pay the price. Years ago, I sacrificed a marriage, underwent a few months of change and transition and gained personal freedom. I'll do with my life what *I* feel is right and what *I* want. That realization gives me peace and a good measure of joy. And even if I marry again, I may make sacrifices out of love, but I'll never again sacrificed myself."

And think not you can direct the course of love, for love, if it finds you worthy, directs your course..... let these be your desires... To know the pain of too much tenderness..... To wake at dawn with a winged heart and give thanks for another day of loving; To rest at the noon hour and meditate love's ecstacy; To return home at eventide with gratitude; And then to sleep with a prayer for the beloved in your heart and a song of praise upon your lips...

Kahlil Gibran from *The Prophet*

Right in the Sight of God

If you aren't religious, you may want to skip this section.

Using the surveys I received from severely battered women, I'd like to make another point. These women were told by church leaders, members and their 'religious' families that the only biblical ground for divorce was adultery.

Because they feared certain damnation of their souls, some of them remained in their marriages for years, waiting until they could prove their spouses had committed adultery. They endured extreme physical and mental abuse and allowed their children to be damaged emotionally. Many batterers themselves are 'respected' members of a church.

Through narrow minded, egotistical opinion, God is imposed crucially into the marriage state by mortals to the level of asininity. God is mentioned in most wedding ceremonies and most take place with a religious figure present. Marriage is thought of as a divine union more frequently than it is thought of as a life choice. Scriptures are used to chastise and control religious people if they even consider divorce.

Divorce is a popular focal point for churches. Church leaders like to belabor acts and rituals, things they can see and describe with their reasoning minds. It's easy to avoid the 'sin' of initiating a divorce. And they like to find things of which they aren't guilty so they'll feel better about themselves. This is one facet of organizational self-glorification.

By organizational self-glorification, I mean practices such as expounding upon the virtues of the church and its members, either individually or as a whole and in contrast, condemning others, in general or in particular, using numbers, attendance counts, new member acquisition announcements, contributions, etc., to keep score of the church's success and devising services and social activities to gratify and appease members and increase membership. These are symptoms of mortal self-worship and have little to do with the worship of God.

In all churches, there are spiritually constricted as well as spiritually dependent individuals, probably in about the same ratio as those who aren't in churches. Unfortunately, because they're egotistical and controlling, spiritually constricted individuals frequently seek roles as church leaders. We listen to the minds (opinions) of those who proclaim themselves to be spiritual when actually they're only outwardly religious and have no real concept of the spirit themselves.

Attending a christian college, majoring in theology and/or being able to quote scripture with astounding accuracy is no assurance of Godly sanctification. The devil can quote scripture with astounding accuracy. He uses it to fulfill his purpose. His purpose is to destroy our soul. If your spirit, your soul has been troubled by your marriage for years, ignore human interference and hear what your spirit tells you.

Hypocrisy is rampant in churches everywhere and is condemned more than any other thing in the bible. It's the only thing we have record of Christ becoming angry about. And yet we hear more sermons condemning divorce, including pro-marriage ones, than we do hypocrisy. Not only are we seldom discouraged from being religious hypocrites, we're *encouraged* to be hypocrites were our marriages are concerned.

People have the best intentions, but by fostering the suppression and oppression of your soul under the guise of marriage, they may be unknowingly serving an evil purpose. Marriage shouldn't be a lifelong test filled with temptations we can't withstand. Preoccupation with and bondage to a bad marriage may be preventing you from fulfilling your Godly purpose.

I believe our spirits, the most important component of ourselves, existed before our minds and bodies and will continue to exist after our minds and bodies are gone. The bible indicates we are endowed with many spirits and that we are also connected to each other by being units of One

Spirit. God gives us the Holy Spirit, the Spirit of Truth to guide us in everything we do. (John 16:13) We are told we will be baptized, or immersed in and washed clean by the Holy Spirit. (Mark 1:8)

Baptism by water takes place when we choose. Baptism by the Holy Spirit takes place when God chooses. There is no indication that these events always take place simultaneously as they did in a few dramatic biblical accounts. In my experience and in the experience of those I know, Spiritual baptism takes years, prayers and is ongoing, much like the growing and maturing of our physical and mental selves.

The crucifixion of Christ is a dramatic parallel example of how inferior mortal mind control must be eventually put to death in order for Spiritual supremacy to culminate. His crucifixion was a painful but voluntary sacrifice of one constrictive way of life in exchange for a supernal one.

In the same way, our Spirit grows until our mortal body is destroyed by death. Our Spirit then becomes our total being. Ideally it has been made stronger and more

127

perfect during our time of mortality. We've accomplished this by learning to be Spiritually dependent. It's evidenced by our love for God, others and ourselves, faith in a higher power, hope for eternal life and a hunger for truth.

Instead of reaching this ideal, we may become dependent on our minds and the minds of others for guidance. We argue our Spirit into a holding cell and close the door. It still tries to communicate with us but we've learned to ignore it, deny its existence and justify what we do with reason and logic.

We don't know what's missing from our lives, we only know something is. We feel bottled up, oppressed and limited in all we do, especially in giving and receiving love. We're burdened, pre-occupied, confused and sad. We don't know what's true and what isn't. Because of repeated disappointments, we don't trust ourselves or others.

Without the guidance of the Spirit, we make bad decisions and become even more unhappy. We seek the help of learned minds. They give us ineffective advice and/or drugs, expecting cause and effect solutions. Unless they are truly spiritual themselves and can help us free our spirits, their success is limited.

Though it isn't created to be evil, our mind is more easily influenced by evil if our Holy Spirit is restricted. Perhaps this is what is meant in the second and third chapters of Revelation by "he who overcomes." Either the Spirit or the mind will overcome and govern. We have the power to decide which.

During our lifetime, a battle much like the battle of Armageddon ensues between our egotistical mind and our Spirit. It goes on inside us through inner conflict, until the Spirit, which is good, or the egotistical mind, which is influenced by evil, prevails. It's difficult for us to choose sides and aid in the victory if we can't tell one side from the other.

Amazing things happen when we set our Spirit completely free and follow it's lead. We live by faith in its awesome capabilities. We feel little fear or inner conflict. Outer conflict hardly affects us. We're able to love others because we don't feel obligated or qualified to judge them anymore. And we know that loving them doesn't require us to endure them. In fact, it's easier for us to love them if we don't endure them.

Though we're taught differently, the bible does *not* say that all marriages are ordained by God. Considering the worst ones, it isn't even logical to think they are. The bible does not say marriage is *always* right and divorce *is always* wrong in God's eyes or that when we wed, God joins us together. Only mortals say that using garbled scriptural interpretations as a basis.

Who could know what God ordains or joins together unless He tells us? How can sexual intercourse and a legal document represent divine union? The problem is that we don't wait for God to join us to anyone. We become impatient, grab the first person who qualifies and do it ourselves.

Because a person, whom other persons have ordained, conducts the ceremony, doesn't mean God gives blanket approval of every ritual. It seems we arrogantly expect God to ordain on command simply because we say, "Okay, God, we're having a wedding here, ordain it." He knows our marriages are bad before we speak the first vow. He doesn't have to punish us for being stupid. We exact our own punishment.... years of it.

Ideally a marriage should be all the things God intended it to be. If it were, it would indeed be a sin for anyone to put it asunder or break it apart. Unfortunately, the ones putting most marriages asunder are the same ones who mistakenly joined it together, the husband and/or the wife. It only takes one, and the breaking apart comes long before the divorce.

When God speaks of marriage and divorce, he's addressing those who are love deficient (spiritually constricted) and those who indulge in 'legal' bed hopping. Bed hoppers are the ones who usually, but not always, obtain a divorce and remarry between hops. We all know, just as God does, that they're merely changing partners every few years. He tells them not to excuse themselves by observing formalities. He's saying sexual immorality is wrong no matter how legal you try to make it.

I'm not suggesting you ignore the bible. I believe the bible is divinely inspired, but I believe it is largely misinterpreted and presented to us with scant spiritual influence. It contains many contradictions. It isn't the infallible Word of God we're conditioned to believe. It's the Word of God written by men, translated by men, and with a few choice words of men interjected here and there to make the meanings 'conform'.

In the book of Revelations we're warned not to add to or take away from its content. If this scripture refers to the whole bible, the taking away and adding to has already been done on a grand scale. Entire books have been removed from the original text.

It's human nature to claim divine inspiration to validate mortal opinion and control others. Church leaders and scholars, mortal men, gave us the bible we have today. If you haven't done so, read any history of the bible.

To add to the confusion, one language cannot be literally translated to another. For many phrases and words the best a translator can do is offer a 'something like' word or phrase. Mortal interference is the reason we have so many different English translations of the same book and even more interpretations of those translations.

Biblical scripture has complex meaning. It can be

applied individually and universally. To interpret it literally instead of spiritually is like looking at the surface of a rock and not realizing there's gold in the center. Commandments given were to show us the ideal, the best possible way. Try reading every command saying "ideally" as the first word.

In essence, the bible is an invaluable general guide to a spiritual life, not a literal guide to a mortal one. It isn't a follow-to-the-letter book of complicated rules and rituals imposed upon us by a punitive God. It's a book of exhortation to spirituality and peace, a blessing from a loving Power. The Power of Love. We cannot begin to understand it unless we understand spirituality.

Because of hardened hearts God gave the followers of Moses a way out of marriage through divorce. He didn't intend for hearts to be hardened, minds to be closed or spirits to be constricted, but He knows they are. We have hardened hearts today and He has given us the same way out.

God knows us better than we know ourselves. Christ lived as a mortal to show God what mortals are like.

He also showed us what God is like. God judges each of us individually, as Christ did, with wisdom, mercy and love. He doesn't name groups for all-inclusive condemnation and give other mortals special privy to naming those groups.

I can't picture Christ thundering, "Behold! All you who are divorced without cause of adultery, separate yourselves to the left, stand on that quaking ground and wait for the harsh judge! And those of you who remarried, go straight to hell!"

We, with God's help, must determine the effect our marriage has on our Spirits and the Spirits of those we love. What good purpose does it serve? We can boldly do this without fear of mortal judgement. Mortals are not qualified to judge. If they do, they are the ones who are wrong.

Ideally we should do all things out of love, especially marry or remain in a marriage. Other than the one we have with God, marriage is the longest lasting and closest relationship of our lives. If God is love, and our marriage is void of love, then it is also void of God. If it's continually provoking us to anger, frustration, hatred and contention no matter how we try to prevent it, how can God condone it? If we give love and it receives little or no responsive replenishing, our spirits tell us to walk away or we'll be drained.

Jesus knew when to leave conflict and when his staying would serve a Godly purpose. He loved all people but He didn't waste valuable time tolerating or sustaining relationships with closed minded, spiritually constricted ones. His Spirit guides us to do the same.

Every moment is a new beginning. Invite Peace.
Go where your spirit leads you.
It can see forever...

☞ ♂ ♀ ☜

ORDER FORM

Estuary Publishing
P. O. Box 1431
Dickson, TN 37056-1431
Fax: (615) 446-2912

Ship to:

Name:_____

Address:_____

City/State/Zip:_____

Phone:_____

Title:	Qty:	Price ea.	Total:
_____			
_____			
_____			
_____			

OrderTotal:_____

Ground mail shipping will be paid by publisher. Allow 4-6 weeks for delivery. For orders of 3-10 books deduct 20% - 10-200 deduct 35% - 200+ deduct 50%. Books may be returned for a full refund.

Payment by: MO_____   CK_____   MC_____   Visa_____

Card Number: ☐☐☐☐ ☐☐☐☐ ☐☐☐☐ ☐☐☐☐

Name on card:_____

Expiration date:_____

ORDER FORM

Estuary Publishing
P. O. Box 1431
Dickson, TN 37056-1431
Fax: (615) 446-2912

Ship to:

Name:_____

Address:_____

City/State/Zip:_____

Phone:_____

Title:	Qty:	Price ea.	Total:
_____	____	_____	_____
_____	____	_____	_____
_____	____	_____	_____
_____	____	_____	_____

OrderTotal:_____

Ground mail shipping will be paid by publisher. Allow 4-6 weeks for delivery. For orders of 3-10 books deduct 20% - 10-200 deduct 35% - 200+ deduct 50%. Books may be returned for a full refund.

Payment by: MO_____   CK_____   MC_____   Visa_____

Card Number: ☐☐☐☐ ☐☐☐☐ ☐☐☐☐ ☐☐☐☐

Name on card:_____

Expiration date:_____